The
Entrepreneur's Identity
Standard

The Entrepreneur's Identity Standard

What entrepreneurs think about themselves and how it influences their entrepreneurial actions

TATIANA KUKOVA, PhD

eBooks2go

Your Author Journey Begins Here

Quantity Purchases:
Companies, professional groups, clubs, and other organizations
may qualify for special terms when ordering quantities of this title.
For information, email info@ebooks2go.net,
or call (847) 598-1150 ext. 4141.
www.ebooks2go.net

Published in the United States
by eBooks2go, Inc.
1827 Walden Office Square, Suite 260, Schaumburg, IL 60173

Paperback ISBN: 978-1-5457-5272-2
Hardcover ISBN: 978-1-5457-5281-4

Library of Congress Cataloging in Publication

To my Mum and Dad: I know that I am
the apple of your eye.

To all my entrepreneurs:
I wanted to give something back.

CONTENTS

Introduction

TO SET THE WHEELS IN MOTION

The most important CEO skill is to be able to manage his own psychology.

–BEN HOROWITZ

Dear Start-up Entrepreneur,

I can't help but start with the most recent events caused by the COVID-19 world pandemic at the beginning of 2020. Following the evidence offered by academics and professional researchers from the national Enterprise Research Centre UK, the country was already in recession by May 2020, which seemed to be a global trend.

On the one hand, small and medium-sized enterprises or companies (SMEs) attracted much attention because of how the economic shutdown had affected their trade. SMEs included bars, restaurants, cafes, day spas and wellness centres, beauty salons, small local shops, bakeries, and other establishments in the form of franchisees. Baking from home became the new normal for a markedly large population. On the other hand, high-tech start-ups were less visible to the general public. Despite that, the shutdown had profoundly changed their operations, urging founders to rethink their business models.

Following *This Week in Start-Ups,* a US weekly podcast hosted by Jason Calacanis, most founders had cut their salaries by 50 to 80 per cent or had decided to continue their day-to-day operations with no pay. Furthermore, many employees had lost their jobs – and this is regardless of whether tech or non-tech companies employed them.

According to *Wired UK,* by autumn 2020, even more employees are going to lose their jobs, small start-ups will shut down, and investors will be short of capital because of their failed investments. It appears that new start-ups may require more cash in the months ahead.

In a nutshell, the picture is gloomy for many tech start-up founders and small business owners. Also reported by *Wired UK,* tech giants, including Uber Eats, Just Eat, and Deliveroo have already felt the full extent of the crisis on their bottom lines. This downturn also accounts for strategic partnerships these companies have with McDonald's, KFC, Subway, and Wagamama. It is also undoubtedly true regarding the health and safety of their staff and products. As you may have seen, these are not the only examples from the food delivery market.

This means that there are fewer customers than usual, which affects customer financing, often referred to as revenue or sales revenue – a considerable chunk of which has already disappeared in a flash. However, this is not the only outcome. No wonder employers and employees are under a lot of stress and pressure, which might lead to anxiety and various other psychological challenges.

The book you have just opened is entitled 'The Entrepreneur's Identity Standard: What entrepreneurs think about themselves and how it influences their entrepreneurial actions.' I've done it for a number of reasons.

First and foremost, I believe that *The Entrepreneur's Identity Standard* solves the psychological problem of how you deal with strategic decision-making processes in your start-up, especially in the current climate. Consequently, it creates value by explaining what the 'entrepreneur's identity' is and why it is of considerable significance to you to be aware of it.

Secondly, I genuinely believe that my ideas are innovative and worth spreading because I base *The Entrepreneur's Identity Standard* on a pioneering doctoral study which I conducted at one UK technology start-up incubator a few years ago. That opportunity allowed me to spend the most enjoyable time with tech start-up founders. My pioneering doctoral research was the foundation for the 2015-2017 United Kingdom Science and Technology Parks Survey (UKSTP Survey) conducted by academics at Aston Business School in Birmingham, UK. That is why this is a personal book where I want to engage your interest from the first few pages.

Therefore, this book is of service to you. Whether you are a student, a first-time founder, a serial entrepreneur, or an investor who works with start-ups, this will be a breakthrough book for you, as it rationalises the social psychology behind the role of the entrepreneur and their actions. I am eager to share with you what the start-up founders revealed to me about themselves to make you understand how that influenced their strategic choices inside and outside their ventures.

Furthermore, I believe that *The Entrepreneur's Identity Standard* will challenge you to rethink how you see others, including investors, executive team members, other start-up founders, and employees. It will help you adjust how you reach your decisions accordingly.

I also believe that *The Entrepreneur's Identity Standard* will advance your knowledge, improve your judgement, and perfect your character. It seems that the booming high-tech industries across the world urgently require this type of entrepreneurial talent.

Perhaps most crucially, I am fond of practical examples, so you'll see them in abundance in my book. Some of them are general. Most of them, however, are grounded in my research data, which show how tech start-up founders make strategic decisions based on their identity.

I have removed academic jargon and a rather vague wording for simplicity, since I trust that different sectors can apply the ideas of *The Entrepreneur's Identity Standard* in their leadership practice.

I should highlight that the names of all entrepreneurs in this book are pseudonyms. It has been done on purpose to disguise the real identities of the start-up founders because of the data protection regulations (the UK Data Protection Act, 1998).

Finally, I fervently believe that this book will be well worth your attention.

Yours truly,
Dr Tatiana Kukova
July 2020

Chapter 1

THE GIST

I've never thought of myself as a female engineer, or founder, or a woman in tech. I just think of myself as someone who's passionate.

–LEAH BUSQUE

This is a book about how entrepreneurs see themselves. I base my writings on face-to-face interviews that I carried out with start-up entrepreneurs at the UK's digital tech incubator as part of my doctoral research programme.

Don't be alarmed: it is not an academic book! My interview interactions just provided fresh insights into what start-up founders thought about themselves and their strategic actions or choices. That is why the ideas in this book are about the entrepreneur's identity — consequently, the entrepreneur's identity standard.

Just to put the record straight: I do not predict the entrepreneurs' actions or decisions or strategic choices. Instead, I explain how the founders act or make decisions or strategic preferences. Later in this chapter, I will explain to you the critical distinction which I draw between behaviour and actions.

Basis of the entrepreneur's identity and its operation

In this section, I want to give you the basics. First and foremost, 'identity' is a concept that points to a set of meanings that represents an individual in three different ways. For instance:

1. How he or she sees themselves in a *role* (e.g., a start-up founder, a CEO, an entrepreneur, an angel investor, a venture capitalist (VC), a retired VC, an intern, a research scientist, a product manager, an engineer, a data analyst, but also a father or mother, a brother or sister, a good friend, a member of a sports club, or a neighbour). As academics point out, identities link to roles that exist within the social structure.

2. How he or she sees themselves in a *social situation* or a particular *social group* (e.g., American or British, male or female, or a member of the Green Party).

3. How he or she sees themselves as an *individual* (e.g., easy-going, moral, honest or dishonest, cunning, witty, trustworthy, determined, or ambitious).

I apply the term 'entrepreneur's identity' to an individual engaged in entrepreneurship. For example, Mark is an entrepreneur, but you may also think of him as a husband or partner, a father, a brother, and a member of a sports club.

I'll give you another example. Sofia is a start-up founder. Despite that, she is also a graduate, the only daughter in her family, and a cheerful person. Consequently, all individuals have multiple identities. That is why the meanings of 'identity' are social in their nature. In other words, any social situation creates these meanings for an individual.

For scientists, the entrepreneur's identity is inseparable from roles as a motivating factor to engage in entrepreneurship. I view 'entrepreneurship' as an activity of starting and running a business with the help of various resources. In my opinion, an entrepreneur is an individual who realises there is an opportunity out there and takes actions despite possible risks. This book is a practical guide to better understand entrepreneurs in their start-up environment according to their roles.

Let's imagine these circumstances. The board of directors decides to push a CEO out of their role in a venture. In other words, to fire them and find a new, more suitable in their view replacement for the role of the CEO. Our former CEO goes to a social event where others ask questions about their current position or plans: 'Who are you now? What do you do? What do you want to do?' As you may guess, this is a thoroughly unpleasant situation for the individual. 'What is the cause of that?' you may ask. It seems to be because their identity has been affected: the lost sense of who one is. Nobody wants *others* to put them down or humiliate them in front of everybody else. It is quite apparent that a vast majority of people will be reluctant to talk about what happened: mull events over. And this is obvious: comments from other people may psychologically hurt.

To better grasp the identity of an entrepreneur, I want you to familiarise yourself with the concept of 'identity' as a system, or a 'feedback loop', consisting of four components: the input perceptions, the identity standard, the comparator, and the output to the social situation. I will now take each of them in turn.

First are the 'input perceptions' of self-relevant meanings from the situation of interaction, which include both how the individual sees him or herself (individual's perceptions) and how others see him or her (also called 'reflected appraisals'). What do *others* believe the entrepreneur should do in their role?

By 'others' I mean other entrepreneurs, angel investors and VCs, employees, vendors, business partners, and other stakeholders who have a vested interest in the start-up. How do they see that entrepreneur? For example, comments from *others* about the lost CEO position when others talk about him or her. The self-relevant meanings are about the entrepreneur because they are only relevant to them – they are about their identity. The self-relevant meanings are about who the entrepreneur is in that role.

Second is the 'entrepreneur's identity standard' – the subjective meanings of that identity. What does the entrepreneur think he or she should do in a particular position, and how does he or she view themselves in that role? For instance, how the entrepreneur sees him or herself as an entrepreneur, an owner, a founder, a co-founder, or a leader. What is so special about a founder – and maybe a CEO position – for the entrepreneur personally? What do entrepreneurs think about it when they hold it? Also, what does the entrepreneur think *others* should do in their roles in a start-up? How do they hire people, and what do they feel about them?

My answer to all these questions is that the entrepreneur's identity standard manifests itself in the entrepreneur's actions: it is the core of the entrepreneur's identity. That is why they perform a particular action. That is why they think about *themselves* and *others* in a certain way.

I want to illustrate this point with one example. What does the entrepreneur think about him or herself when signing a term sheet with an investor? My observation would be that the entrepreneur's identity and the entrepreneur's identity standard of motivations would shine through when negotiating the terms of this agreement (i.e. term sheet provisions). The actual signing of documents is the action of the entrepreneur. They direct this action towards the term sheet because they do what's right for them from their perspective. What the entrepreneurs think is right for them always refers to their identity standard of motivations first. The bottom line is that this identity standard will come into play with the 'how' and 'what' they are signing.

I use the word 'action' for the entrepreneur in the context of what they are *doing* or what they *can do* based on how they think about themselves in a particular fashion. I seldom refer to the word 'behaviour' because it is often about opinions or comments expressed, values communicated, questions, and gestures. 'Action' is a much stronger word than 'behaviour' and therefore more accurate. The environment that surrounds the entrepreneur serves as the action's context. They usually direct their efforts towards a particular mission, or purpose, or goal.

Consider the following situation. A CEO has demoted or is inclined to downgrade one of the members of his executive team. Let's assume that the CEO directs this action towards a bigger purpose in mind: improvement of the overall company's performance and long-term survival. However, the way to do this would depend on the CEO's identity standard. For example, his or her love of power. It is a clear manifestation of the CEO's identity. The consequences of the reduction in rank or status would depend on what feels comfortable to the CEO, and whether or not he or she thinks about *others* in the company and their inevitable reactions following the CEO's decision. This example shows the CEO's true colours because it reveals their identity standard of power.

Third is the 'comparator' – the mechanism that operates to compare the inputs from the environment with the identity-standard meanings. To put this differently, how the entrepreneur's head takes the situation and compares it with a deeply ingrained identity standard of some sort before undertaking any action.

Fourth is the 'output' to the environment or social situation in the form of meaningful social behaviour based on the difference between the self-relevant perceptions and the meanings held in the identity standard. In other words, what you say and do in a given situation. What will you tell them about your CEO position? Will you tell the real story: the story behind the story, as it were?

Four types of disturbances

We can now talk about 'disturbances' or 'interruptions' because they are critical to the entrepreneur's identity. These may be *external events*, such as tech conferences, rising start-up pitch competitions, meetings with a mentor, various kinds of communication with vendors, meetings with partners, networking events, and other types of events. For example, a start-up founder finds themselves at a tech conference they do not want to be at because they think they are wasting their time. Such an event is a disturbance for them. It is also a significant disturbance to the meanings that they have about themselves and about what they really should be doing.

Other roles or identities could be a source of disturbance: identities within the individual. For example, the entrepreneur identity and the parent or spouse identity may conflict with one another. 'How can I be a successful entrepreneur and a good father?' one might think. In this case, the third description would kick in.

Here is what I mean: if an entrepreneur holds tightly to his or her entrepreneur's identity, any disturbance from another identity – father or mother or partner – will be unthinkable. Adverse emotional reactions, worries or anxieties are inevitable. However, if an entrepreneur does not hold tightly to his or her identity as an entrepreneur, he or she will allow the disturbances to occur and will not respond to them as strongly. 'All right, I think I can be a decent parent and a successful entrepreneur,' they may tell themselves.

The third type is interruptions by *periodic* or *episodic identities*. As the name suggests, they activate during a particular period. When identity activates, it means it is in operation. For example, when a founder or CEO has to appear in the media but does not like it. One possibility may be because they consider it to be another role for them. Some entrepreneurs may allude to the fact that media appearances boost a company's image. Others disagree on the grounds that such events do not directly relate to day-to-day operations inside a start-up. They even call it 'being a fake CEO'. If you think about it, this uncomfortable identity in our example is periodic and in operation for a short period. Nevertheless, it is undoubtedly an interruption for the founder.

The final type of disturbances is the disturbances from *other individuals*, such as other start-up founders, investors, mentors, partners, vendors, employees, and other stakeholders. 'What do they think about me and my performance?' an entrepreneur might think. If a start-up founder has a good relationship with an investor who happens to be candid, trustworthy, and reliable, each individual's identity supports the identity of the other. These are 'mutually relevant identities' because both of them verify the meanings they hold about themselves in their identity standard of how the relationships between a founder and an investor should look. One is happy to work with the other, which confirms the identity-standard meanings they hold for each other. 'He is a pleasure to work with,' one can think to themselves. 'He knows what I am going through, and he is eager to help me. He is the one I can trust,' an entrepreneur might think about their investor.

I want to make one thing abundantly clear for you: the problem is not whether entrepreneurs verify or not verify their identity standard of, say, success. In essence, the problem is their actions afterwards. Naturally, it is nice to work with people who have similar identity standard to your own because their thoughts and justifications of these thoughts will be close to your heart. Most problems arise because of the opposite scenario. For example, when an investor has an entirely different view about money than an entrepreneur. Lack of alignment or the total absence of it will ultimately lead to identity non-confirmation on both sides. Therefore, it may result in all sorts of challenging behaviours and indecisive leadership. For instance, potentially confusing term sheets which work solely to the investor's advantage.

A real-world story

At this point, I would like to describe to you an excerpt from a publicly available conversation between Sam Altman and Craig Cannon from the YC podcast of 8th November 2018 before delving into the examples from my doctoral research data. You may be wondering who the people I have just mentioned are. Here is their quick biography.

Sam Altman is a CEO of OpenAI LP and former president of Y Combinator, and Craig Cannon is a former director of marketing at Y Combinator (YC) and a legendary host of YC podcasts. YC is the most famous seed accelerator and fund for tech start-ups in Silicon Valley. The whole conversation is available online, and this is what Sam had to say that intrigued me about the entrepreneur's identity and the entrepreneur's identity standard:

> Let me try to frame in like in an area when a lot of things went wrong at once but in a way that was really good. So I sold my start-up when I was like twenty-six or something like that … and then I took a year off. And in that year (which is hard to do, it is really hard to do in Silicon Valley). Because in a place where social status is determined by your job and what you are working on. Like … when, you show up at a party, and someone says, "What are you working on?" and you are like, "Ah. I am kind just taking the year off." You can, sort of, see in real-time their eyes like look for someone else in the room to talk to. Doesn't feel that good. But it's an incredibly privileged thing to be able to do this.

And then he added:

> But if you are in the position between jobs when you can take a year off – I highly recommend it. I think it was like one of the two or three best career things that I ever did. In that year, I read like many dozens of textbooks, I learned about fields that I had been interested in. I didn't have any idea that they would all come together in the way they did: I learned a lot about nuclear engineering, a lot about AI … I learned about investing. I travelled around a lot

and really got a feel for … what the rest of the world is like. I met people that were working on all sorts of different things that were nice enough to talk to me. I had time to reconnect with my friends and family – just caught up on life. I helped people; I had unlimited time.

From my perspective, this is the case of two different identity standards of success: Sam's and the other (let's assume that the social situation involved one person). It was natural for Sam to take a year off in pursuit of other activities, such as reading books and learning about early-stage investing. The other person, however, did not want to take him seriously and treat him with genuine respect. On the contrary, he or she tried to find some other entrepreneurs in order to benefit from networking perhaps. In their eyes, Sam did not have the "preferred" status in Silicon Valley.

It is a clear case when the meanings in the other's identity standard of success are closely intertwined with status, perhaps high status, such as working for Google, Facebook, Amazon, or Apple. This status most likely connects with prestige and personal advancement or gain. There were no positive connotations of taking a year off in their identity standard of success. They could even have thought of it as a failure with limited prospects – certainly not what they planned or calculated for themselves in their head. They could also think that Sam was just foolish or naïve enough to proceed further rather than take on a new, more powerful and influential role or position in society. Ultimately, what these people did not seem to realise was that they were utterly transparent in their total absence of morals. If this is an attitude towards a successful entrepreneur who had sold his company, you may guess the behaviour towards other yet unknown entrepreneurs.

There are a variety of reasons why *others* could afford themselves to misbehave. If they had known about their standard at the time, would they have behaved in that fashion? Oh yes, without question, because they would not have believed these were the meanings in their identity standard of success. In their view, 'success' meant achieving a formal status or securing a formal title, such as founder, CEO, co-founder, COO, CTO, engineer, VP, angel investor and mentor, or partner at a VC firm. These *others* would have called it rational reasoning and good sense. Beneath the surface, however, they would have laughed at non-formal titles. Being immersed in their identity standard of success, they would not have understood Sam's logic under any circumstances.

For Sam, on the other hand, it was the right decision or strategic choice because his skills seemed to have improved immensely. Despite trying various projects which did not end up in success, he saw the value of his activities and perfected himself as an entrepreneur, and even as an investor. In his head, he was successful and confirmed his identity standard of success by deriving much pleasure from his year off. Despite feelings of unease, discomfort, and awkwardness when he faced that *other* at the party, he knew the effectiveness of his actions.

By taking the above example of Sam Altman, I wanted to depict the most typical disrespectful behaviour towards one's status – or the total absence of it – in a social situation. Remember, it is the operation of the identity standard of success in the head of the *other* as well as Sam's that requires confirmation. Before blaming others, look closely at the operation of their identity as I have just demonstrated to you. It will help you move forward in the right direction and not spend a considerable amount of time mulling over different social situations in your head. Events are fleeting. Wait for another one. By sharpening your attention, other entrepreneurs, partners, and investors will not annoy you as much. 'Ah, this is their identity standard of success,' you may catch yourself thinking.

Because disturbances are beyond individual control, they influence the identity process by altering social situations. Entrepreneurs control the perceptions in the situation to match these meanings to ones they hold in their identity standard. If *others* act as a disturbance by saying something or working in a way which does not resonate with the entrepreneur, the founder does not confirm their own opinion about themselves. 'So what?' you may wonder. Well, the entrepreneur will try to alter their behaviour until their thoughts are consistent with those from the situation about him or herself. They will do their best to prove others wrong. 'Others are wrong about me,' entrepreneurs may say, 'I will show them who I am.'

Positive feelings will be a result of identity-verification or the situation when the entrepreneur confirms how they see themselves. In contrast, negative emotions will point to identity non-verification or the case when the entrepreneur does not endorse their thoughts about themselves. When entrepreneurs receive funding, for example, they verify their identity by feeling good about themselves and their business idea. They satisfy their identity standard of success, as it were. That is why the identity verification process produces positive feelings.

General examples

Let's consider other situations which may occur in the life of a founder. Maybe an entrepreneur who has not built a unicorn company is not considered to be a real entrepreneur. In essence, other entrepreneurs already view them as unsuccessful because of the meanings they hold in their identity standard of success. In other words, because of how they define their identity standard of success or what success means to them personally.

Perhaps an intern is too low in a social hierarchy of roles to respect them. A founder and the CEO of a start-up may think the same way. The output to the social situation will determine how the CEO behaves towards the intern. If they are too low in the CEO's or founder's identity-standard meanings, be prepared for disrespectful and unfair behaviour. The intern may experience unpleasant comments, various jokes, and self-satisfied smirks from such a boss.

Given this, people behave towards other people based on the meanings in their identity standard about others in their roles. To make this even more concrete, imagine a young founder in his twenties who may be treated like a child by a VC because that's how the VC sees the new founder is his role. These are the meanings formed in their identity standard about that young person. 'Why does it matter?' you may be thinking. It matters because of the behaviour and attitude of the VC towards the young founder. Why should we care about the VC's identity-standard meanings? Because they affect the decisions and actions of the VC concerning that founder.

Why is it still relevant? It is crucial, especially for the young founder in our case, since they may know what to do next if they understand the VC's identity standard. For example, they may decide to change the VC, find a new mentor, or pitch angels for other types of support. When you start observing this behaviour and comprehend the essence of it, you will know what to do next. To emphasise this point further, the utilisation of resources is different once you know the identity standard of another person.

What you have just seen are the identities, which are also composed of meanings that others create for that identity. This is because the entrepreneur or others respond to the meanings conveyed by a particular behaviour (i.e., gestures and comments) or a specific action. And that action should match the identity meanings, or the expectations attributed to it.

I want to take another example. Imagine two teams: one is artificial intelligence (AI), and another is information technology (IT) in a unicorn company. Their mindsets differ considerably because AI guys think scientifically and apply different methods to create a new product. IT guys have an established model of behaviour to deliver on their objectives. Not only do these two teams vary in their abilities, knowledge, and skill sets, but they also differ in their identity standard of how to be successful in their roles as research scientists and data scientists.

On the other end of the spectrum, the identity standard of IT professionals will not relate to measuring, testing, and hypothesising based on data. Instead, their focus shifts towards other actionable, often predetermined steps. Therefore, their identity standard of how they see themselves in particular roles will relate to the way they behave in their department.

Tension will inevitably arise between the two teams because of the reasons which I have just explained. Furthermore, it will affect the results brought to the chief technology officer (CTO).

IT guys certainly do not think about their roles as scientific roles, whereas AI guys do. That's all there is to it.

As soon as a particular identity activates in a social situation, the identity process establishes itself. Consequently, all situationally self-relevant meanings as an input to the system are being controlled by it. It is essential to remember, though, that not all the identities activate at the same time.

Consider this situation: a founder is given a slot at a tech conference. The founder identity is the one that is likely to dominate this tech conference. If you think about it, however, being a mentor and a founder at the same time may activate the mentor identity as well.

A married couple that decides to set up a venture and have numerous conversations at home about their future strategy is one more case in point. Under these circumstances, both of their identities get activated: the spouse identity and the founder and the co-founder identity. Drama! I would advise against interfering with the domestics!

I can't resist giving you a bonus example. The time is 2 a.m. An entrepreneur calls their investor and mentor in a panic because the iterations on a product do not produce positive results. Under these circumstances, an investor identity and a mentor identity may activate in a flash because of a genuine desire to help.

I believe you have grasped by now that what one thinks about him or herself defines their identity. It represents the meanings of the roles they have – the meanings they give to themselves. It is their identity standard. Consequently, the entrepreneur forms their opinions or preferences based on the identity standard of self-constructed meanings: the meanings that he or she create themselves. These *meanings* already exist in their identity standard. That is why an individual makes preferences or strategic choices by keeping the standard of their identity in mind.

I should note the feedback from the environment concerns one's identity or self. Following that, it influences what the individual says (i.e. behaviour) and does (i.e. actions) in the situation of interaction.

An error signal

I want you to imagine these circumstances. When iterations on a product do not go according to plan, this does not confirm the identity standard of success or being a successful leader who makes correct decisions. An 'error signal' appears in an individual's head, shouting about failure, unsuccess, or being a looser. This error signal constitutes a difference between input from the environment and the meanings contained in the identity standard.

Most of the time, this error signal produces negativity or negative emotional responses. That is why we can observe panic, irritation, frustration, anger, or similar emotional responses in a founder. Is there anything else? Well, it may lead to disrespectful behaviour or even strategic actions as a sign of defence. The willingness to drop everything and quit, close down the venture, fire somebody, lash out at employees, or invest more energy in what the founder shouldn't in the hope that it will eventually work out.

These examples explain how the error signal in the head modifies the situation. Of course, the circumstances would be different according to what the entrepreneur has in their head. As this operation or thought process in the head is fast, it may result in hasty decisions. Remember, communication with others triggers identity confirmation or identity disconfirmation. When an entrepreneur actively tries to confirm the meanings in their identity standard, they may experience an emotional response. Positive reactions mean that an identity is verified or confirmed. Adverse reactions of all kinds imply that identity is not verified or not confirmed. An individual may hit the roof or cut up rough. As one of the entrepreneurs that I interviewed, Richard, put it:

> I am not a good morning person – better work later on. When I am in a mood, my God, the whole room is in a mood. It's one of those. The *mood* can affect the whole team, really.

Then, he added:

> I don't have patience; I'll be truthfully honest with you. I don't have the patience for stupidity or somebody who is … well …, and you trust him to do a certain job, which then fails. That's my problem. Managing expectations is sometimes tricky for me cause I can't, and we don't have time for it. It's like if we've dropped the ball, and we need to pick it up again.

Identity non-verification may cause or generate negative feelings. Imagine a mismatch between the feedback from others in a particular situation and the identity-standard meanings of that identity — for example, the implications of what success means to an individual. A founder may behave differently to change the perceptions that others have about them. They may say to themselves, 'How others see me is wrong. What they think about me is not true.' It is an attempt to change the negativity of the identity disconfirmation. This situation is likely to happen if the founder has disappointing metrics. As one founder said to me, 'Yeah, it can affect, especially if you take it personally.'

When an entrepreneur defines 'success' in their terms, but the situation is not desirable regarding those terms, the entrepreneur does not see or feel like a success. Again, the identity disconfirmation abounds. As you can imagine, there is even a possibility of unpleasant emotional reactions. In the words of one start-up founder named Scott, who works with distressed business assets (or redundant technologies):

> If I had a couple of thousands of pounds at the end of the day in my pocket, then it would be a successful day. If I had a couple of hundred, then it wouldn't be.

Alternatively, positive feelings will not lead to any changes in actions. It is because the feedback provided by others confirms the identity-standard meanings of success. Have a look at what Matthew from IT and design had to say about that:

> When I raised £20,000 worth of equity for a business that wasn't making any money at the time, you know, people say, "Yeah, you can use all the money." That makes you happy.

What I have described to you so far are general examples, with only a small fraction of doctoral interview data. I did this on purpose to define 'identity', the 'input perceptions' about oneself from the social situation, the 'identity standard', the 'comparator', and the 'output' to the social environment.

I want you to consider this a preamble to the real-world data, which I will lay out for you in the following chapters.

The final points: In the anticipation of data

I was excited to interview the entrepreneurs because I intended to understand the nature of their entrepreneur's identity: that is, their identity standard. For this reason, I asked myself two questions: What do entrepreneurs think about themselves, and how does it influence their entrepreneurial actions? I examined identity concerning the entrepreneur's strategic choices. They were the following: hiring first employees, seeking investors, outsourcing a particular function of the business, building a network, leaving their previous jobs, or deciding to become an entrepreneur in the first place.

I interviewed tech founders from the start-up environment because I wanted to dig deeper. I wanted to discover how the entrepreneur's identity operated in practice. Eventually, I wanted to know what kind of thoughts entrepreneurs secretly held about themselves. I desperately tried to understand how these identity meanings might influence the activities which they carried out.

So, from now on, you can view 'actions' as 'meaningful behaviour' where the 'internal' and 'external' strategic decisions represent the 'actions' of my entrepreneurs. The former was mostly related to the entrepreneur's business practices which arose inside a start-up. The latter referred to the strategic actions connected to the entrepreneur's activities outside the venture. To make it clear and succinct, I have provided my interpretations of the tech entrepreneurs' quotes for each type of these outcomes in Chapters Four and Five.

Chapter 2

MY ENTREPRENEURS

There is a real craft to being a CEO.

–MATT BLUMBERG

It is high time you became familiar with the entrepreneurs I interviewed for my doctoral research. Seed- and early-stage ventures in the digital technology sector represented the chosen pool of my tech start-up founders. These start-ups were mostly pre-revenue, although some founders were already generating some sales revenue. The age of start-up entrepreneurs ranged from 20 to 54 years old. I interviewed the entire cohort – 27 tech founders – enrolled in the tech incubator programme at the time. The team size of the start-ups raged from two-person co-founders to six-person teams, where two or three individuals were co-founders. For instance, Andrew, a first-time entrepreneur in consumer products and energy optimisation, declared:

> There are two directors that work full-time, and then we've got – don't know exactly off the top of my head without counting them – but probably five to six other people that we work with that contribute on a part-time basis. So, some of them are contracted people,

so that's the reason why we are here today cause we are developing a mobile app and we are paying one of the guys here to do that. So, for us, that's contract work. There is a number of people whom we've contracted to do specific projects, and then the other people are sort of volunteering their time on a part-time basis.

Charles, a first-time entrepreneur from the online game and betting sector, shared his views as well:

At the moment, it's just myself and the CTO. So, that CTO is the chief technical officer who is kind of responsible for IT development and then myself. We are looking to get some more graduates on board now, so. But at the moment, it's just the two.

Many of the founders had a team of interns and freelancers because they did not want to employ people full-time at that stage of their venture development. For example, 'So, currently in the office, there are five of us: me, two technical guys, and two interns,' said Patrick, a serial entrepreneur from the video game sector. Ralph, a first-time founder from software for the events industry, put it this way: 'We have a number of freelance developers and associates from time to time in the area between three people to five people depending on what we've got.'

Scott, a serial entrepreneur who worked with redundant technologies, explained his situation:

We have six developers in the business, and we also have some kind of advertising specialists. So, the team – the core team – is just Michael, my co-founder, and me. But the team we've actually worked with is probably about 10 people.

Colin, a serial, versatile entrepreneur whose passions transcended across the education, healthcare, arts, and publishing sectors was pretty much the same: 'There are about seven or eight of us.'

Gregory, who was a serial tech founder in his thirties in the areas of education and IT, pointed out who exactly was on his team: 'We are four founders, one intern, two voluntary teacher-contributors and a couple of junior testers.' I was curious to find out that the people who worked with Gregory were not employees. As he explained, 'I wouldn't say *employees*, but they are part of the group, if you like.' Whereas Reynold, a first-time entrepreneur from social networking, said, 'There are four of us in total with two people being in the office and two people being mobile.'

Luke, a first-time founder from a digital content agency, was considering hiring freelancers on a 'regularish basis'. Carl, also a first-time founder but from a software business, expressed it this way:

> It's just me at the moment. I have hired freelancers in the past and maybe will do it again, but at the moment it's just me. There are no permanent employees rather than me.

Finally, Keith was a seasoned serial entrepreneur who started his first company in the mid-1970s, which was in the 'musical instrument amplifiers and speakers' domain. With a wealth of experience and wisdom, he had his reasons for going solo:

> Team ... that particular business is just me. I set it up after I had quite a successful company, and after about

seven years, we split it up. And then at that point, I started my current company. The idea was to have that as a background company, which would effectively be a way of doing work and creating wealth for myself. And then to alongside that have joint ventures with other people, with other teams as opposed to just a single person. And that's what I've been doing for the last twenty-odd years.

Interestingly, four entrepreneurs had relatively large teams in comparison to the rest of the cohort. Peter, a serial entrepreneur who described his business as just an internet start-up, had a 15-person team, excluding himself as the founder, where he was the only one present at the incubator. Thomas, a serial founder who was working on a mobile app, had an astonishing 28-person team with him and two other interns present. Alan – a serial entrepreneur who worked across several sectors, including technology, training, insurance, and transport – had a 10-person team, where he worked remotely most of the time. Jonathan, a serial entrepreneur with a background in education and technology, had a nine-person team with seven employees, one founder (himself), and one co-founder. And Gregory, a serial entrepreneur who also worked in education and technology but just on a different product, already had 10 people.

Henry, a first-time founder from electronic engineering; Luke, a first-time founder from a digital content agency; and Carl, a first-time entrepreneur, who was developing a software product, decided to work solo. The same applied to Roy, a serial entrepreneur from the hedge fund sector, and Keith, a serial entrepreneur with a software product.

All the tech founders I spoke to were exclusively male and worked full-time on their ventures. The majority of them were from the UK. I conducted my face-to-face interviews in 2013, which was at the outskirts of the emergence of tech incubators and accelerators in the UK. I was a pioneer doctoral researcher who had ever set foot in the UK's technology incubator, which I do not name because of the UK data protection regulations.

I had conversations with founders from various sectors ranging from electronic engineering to the hedge fund sector. Other examples include technology-based retail, gaming, mobile and betting apps, telecommunications and IT software, online marketing, and advertising. Some of the founders were developing technology-related educational materials for children. In contrast, others were building social networking sites for managers. A few of these ventures had already become leading tech start-ups in the city.

At first, I began my interviews with some general questions about the business sector, entrepreneurs' ages, and business history, including the start-up process and how they came up with their business ideas. As you have just seen, I was interested in the size of their teams and whether they ran it full-time or part-time. Then, the questions became more specific, as I was curious about their thinking. For instance, why entrepreneurs thought they were capable of setting up a venture, how they planned activities, the critical milestones in decision-making, and how they searched for new opportunities and people. The topics also included optimism about their start-up process and the factors that motivated them.

Of course, it was crucially important to me to find out how entrepreneurs saw themselves, their definition of 'success', and how involved they were in their tech community. I also asked what reputation meant to them. I encouraged the founders to provide specific examples of their own experiences for greater clarity.

The incubator system and its facilities

The tech incubator was European funded and focused on creating innovative technologies. In the beginning, the incubator members were based in one of the campuses to launch their ventures; then, depending on the companies' growth, they could relocate to larger offices.

To enrol in the incubator programme, individuals had to fill in a short online form to describe a business or a business idea. As I observed when I was on campus, some individuals came with their parents. For instance, a young man came with his dad to talk to the programme manager about his idea and how he could join the incubator.

The manager usually looked for the best fit. They evaluated ideas for start-ups based on their potential and similarity to those who were already on campus. For this reason, prospective members consulted the incubator website to check current companies and alumni members.

There were many benefits that start-up founders derived from being on the incubator programme. They included a co-working centre with full ICT support, meeting facilities, video conferencing equipment, and other technologies. When I was on campus, I could observe how my entrepreneurs shared an open-plan office and hot-desking. According to one of the tech founders there, the office space was designed in the same style as they did at Facebook and Google in Silicon Valley.

On this campus, they adjusted the kitchen to the hot-desking area, which provided an excellent environment for informal conversations and relaxation.

Sometimes I found myself participating in spontaneous talks with some of the cohort. I did this to gain a better understanding of the environment, which later helped me easily picture the hub.

The entrepreneurs could also use their office suites depending on their membership package. For instance, some founders had small offices for one to four people. As I observed, they worked closely with their co-founders and first or early-stage employees. All members enrolled in the incubator programme had access to on-site Café Resource, test labs, meeting rooms, and different events, such as Get Together and Future of Gaming event for digital gaming and mobile app developers.

Informal conversations with the founders made me believe that many of them enjoyed the environment and the incubator community. They also valued an opportunity to present their work to peers at Get Together. Many of them liked an open-plan atrium called Serendipity Street, where they could 'bump into new faces' to create new opportunities for themselves.

It would be no exaggeration to say that my time on campus made me well informed and shrewd about the real entrepreneurs' experiences. That is why I have decided to interpret the founders' quotes related to their identities and share their insights with you. In the chapters that will follow this one, you will find the words from the tech start-up entrepreneurs about what they think about themselves.

Chapter 3

THE ENTREPRENEURS' IDENTITY STANDARD

*Little did they know that I was conspiring to be
their biggest competitor.*

–TONY HSIEH

Entrepreneurs' types

Three types of entrepreneurs have emerged from my scientific data in the form of interviews. 'Success', 'optimism', and 'motivations or capabilities' have been selected for this typology because they represent the identity standard of entrepreneurs. For each of the entrepreneurs in my data set, I charted their levels of optimism, success definitions, and critical founding motivations or capabilities to help me arrive at their identity types. 'Optimism' appears qualitatively different from the other two content aspects of the identity standard, as it seems to refer more to a process dimension – how entrepreneurs behave – while founding 'motivations or capabilities' and 'success' definitions apply to the why. 'Motivations' have been combined with 'capabilities' because the data did not reveal much difference in meaning between the two categories. I use the word 'motivation' in the plural form as 'motivations' because *motivations* come from *motives* when I talk about the entrepreneur's identity.

As the data show, entrepreneurs behave differently based on the variation of their identity standard of success, optimism, and motivations or capabilities. I introduced three "pure" types of entrepreneurs, distinguishing between the 'high-flyers', the 'innovators', and the 'lifestyle' entrepreneurs. The purpose of these types was to simplify and clarify the meanings individuals associated with being an entrepreneur. The difference between the identity standards is a crucial finding of my research because the identity standard of success, optimism, motives or capabilities relate to entrepreneurial actions. Therefore, each of these standards has consequences for entrepreneurial strategies. This finding implies that entrepreneurs may base their strategic decisions on the meanings associated with their identities. Below you can see the descriptions of three types of entrepreneurs' identities and their identity standard of success, optimism, and motivations or capabilities that emerged from my discoveries.

The high-flyers

The first type is the 'high-flyers'. The high-flyers are ambitious individuals who seek to grow their businesses. They will not take *no* for an answer, because they know that it is possible. They want to make a difference in the world by achieving their full potential in entrepreneurial activity. As Roy put it:

> Because maybe I think too much of myself. I am an intelligent guy, or so I like to think. I guess the reason is that it's a challenge. I want freedom. Money combined with freedom. You never know who works

for somebody else makes a billion dollars. It will never happen because you have that dependency.

The high-flyers' identity standard of 'success' pertains to self-development and monetary values as its bases. This type of entrepreneurs is continually learning. They set high goals for themselves and want to reach them against the odds. They have high growth aspirations because they always want more and want to achieve more.

The high-flyers' identity standard of 'optimism' relates to the expression of high levels of optimism. Founders in this category know what they are doing and believe they can reach their goal. Their ambitions come first.

The high-flyers' identity standard of 'motivations or capabilities' manifests itself in having their own business and being able to reach their potential. They are ambitious, and they want high status. Some of them continue the family tradition of running a business because part of their identity is generational.

The innovators

The second type is the 'innovators'. The innovators are the entrepreneurs who are creative and inventive. These individuals are committed to innovation, as they are always looking for new ways of doing things. They are constantly juggling different ideas to be able to innovate. Stanley explained it this way: '… interested in creating things that … passionate about. I get more passionate about working on my own product.' The other entrepreneur named Andrew added: 'I am passionate about the automation side. And it's all about making things more efficient.'

The innovators' identity standard of 'success' is mostly tied to monetary gain – namely, sales revenue with a profit margin and positive cash flow. Their understanding of reputation relates to being known for a venture's product. These entrepreneurs have growth aspirations as part of their identity.

The innovators' identity standard of 'optimism' is about fundamental optimism ingrained in these start-up founders, leading to innovation. In spite of that, they express low levels of confidence about their product.

The innovators' identity standard of 'motivations or capabilities' manifests itself in being artistic and passionate about creating something new. Naturally they love puzzles and enjoy solving problems.

The lifestyle

The third and final type is the 'lifestyle'. The lifestyle entrepreneurs are individuals who seek to execute a business strategy which suits the lifestyle they have already created for themselves. They want to stay in control. At the same time, they need the flexibility to develop their ventures without jeopardising their lifestyle expectations. In the words of Keith:

> With any business, you have to judge it by financial success. The idea of that was doing things I was really interested in doing. So, I judge 'success' as how much time I spend every day doing things I really want to do.

The lifestyle entrepreneurs' identity standard of 'success' is based on financial security and personal independence. They do not have high growth aspirations.

The lifestyle entrepreneurs' identity standard of 'optimism' is usually expressed through realism and ambivalence.

The lifestyle entrepreneurs' identity standard of 'motivations or capabilities' relates to autonomy because these entrepreneurs are constantly looking for independence through setting up their ventures. At the same time, they want continuity of their lifestyle.

Overall, I have built these types of entrepreneurs on what I have discovered about their identity standards. This simplification clarifies the meanings start-up founders associate with being an entrepreneur. Of course, despite these "pure" types, variations still exist within each of these types, so please don't take it as black-and-white. Perhaps you may have met individuals who could have had the characterises of two types or all three. The point of this book is to show you what entrepreneurs think about themselves in a way you can easily understand.

To conclude, the identity standard of start-up founders is the meanings that they give to themselves when they are in the role of the entrepreneur. It is their way of thinking about a particular action, which is inseparable from them as individuals. That is why all the entrepreneur's opinions or preferences or strategic decisions are referred to their identity standard first.

Entrepreneurs' possible decisions

What matters most is that you understand why entrepreneurs act in specific ways and how confirmation or non-confirmation of the identity standard influences their entrepreneurial actions. To put it another way, how verification of their entrepreneurial identity affects their strategic choices.

You may wonder at this point about what kind of 'strategic decisions' or 'strategic choices' or 'strategic preferences' there can be. Let me give you a whole range of examples. These are the decisions that you can typically find in most books written by entrepreneurs for entrepreneurs:

- identifying relevant opportunities which lead to venture creation;
- selecting an appropriate start-up idea;
- focusing on the market above all else;
- going solo at first;
- trying to find a like-minded co-founder with whom you have an aligned set of objectives;
- deciding on how to use start-up resources at hand;
- hiring first employees, including junior (later senior) web and mobile app developers and engineers, programmers, and designers;
- dividing the shares between the executive team members – first employees who are critical to the business's survival – and the investors;
- deciding to expand the team by taking new employees on, including product managers, machine learning specialists, robotics specialists, engineers who can perform profound aspects of scaling serves, marketing and branding experts, and community people[1];
- bootstrapping based on strong financial performance or raising capital from FFF (friends, family, and fools), angel investors, venture capitalists (VCs), or (at a much later stage) corporate venture capitalists (CVCs);

---

[1] I should note that technology incubators often provide legal support and help with accounting. Hence, there is a choice to outsource these business functions.

- securing further rounds of funding;
- developing and improving the product or service;
- getting the first interested customer and growing a user base by understanding who the users are and what they want and need;
- improving the existing marketing strategy and sales;
- finding candid mentors among the board of directors or their networks;
- thinking about the company's mission, vision, and values to create a positive culture within the company;
- deciding what salary and benefits employees should have;
- managing employees' expectations about office hours;
- pivoting by suddenly moving in a new direction, namely creating and launching a new product if the previous one did not live up to customers' expectations; and
- ultimately, creating value by solving a problem.

The list above is not exhaustive, but it provides an informative overview by giving you an idea of the possible strategic decisions that founders need to make at an early or seed stage in a company's life cycle of growth.

As you have learned earlier in this chapter, every entrepreneur has an identity standard of some sort. They may be similar or not. It means that the identity standard of success, optimism, motives or capabilities influence the way entrepreneurs make their business decisions. They have consequences for entrepreneurial strategies. It is true. You may wonder, 'How does it manifest itself?' My answer is this: the tech start-up founders often base their strategic decisions outlined above on the meanings associated with their identities.

Let's take a small example of going solo when setting up a venture. As Henry (an inventor identity) explained, 'Just me at the moment. I will have employees, hopefully, eventually. It will be good.' Luke (the lifestyle entrepreneur identity) gave his reasons:

> Like I said … at the moment, most of the time, it's just me, but I probably have about five freelancers that I use on a regularish basis. It just depends at the moment on how much work I get. What I have been doing up to this point is just get enough work for myself. And when I get too much cause freelancing tends to … all the work seems to come in like one point. He-he-he. It can be quite … you can go for a week with not much work and all ever sudden everyone wants to work. So, I've used outsourcing and freelancers on a fairly regular basis, but now I'm going more down that route of trying to get a lot more work and using those guys on a more regular basis. Yeah.

All the founders that I met were going through the early stage of venture development. During that stage, all of them were trying to develop and promote their business ideas. At the same time, they were starting with their identity standard, which concerned their role as founders and related to the potential of their business idea. Moreover, they were contemplating what 'success' meant to each of them.

You may be thinking, 'Why is it important?' I would say the following in my reply. Not only do entrepreneurs set up their businesses with a possible business concept, but they also start with a clear identity standard of success. This standard consists of a set of their meanings about themselves: the image in their heads about who they think they are. In other words, their role as entrepreneur and thoughts about excellent performance against their meanings of success in that role. They always refer to these meanings in social situations.

'How?' you may be wondering. The comparator in an entrepreneur's head compares the feedback from *others* with these meanings. What others say or do may act as a 'disturbance' or 'interruption' (see Chapter One) for what they think about themselves. As you may guess, that's the real reason why it plays an active role in affecting future outcomes. The comparison happens quickly. There may be an instant reaction to what others say or do. It is the comparator in action: trying to adjust the meanings that others have about the entrepreneur and the entrepreneur's meanings about themselves.

As an analogy, let's think of a tech founder who is engaged in the process of finding co-founders, early employees, and investors to get the business off the ground. To proceed further with this example, let's imagine he or she wants to assemble a team of seven people, working on a full-time or part-time basis in an office. It is possible to assume a variety of disturbances that disrupt the processes away from what the entrepreneur wants it to be. For instance, difficulties in terms of finding people with high-quality human capital, including suitable education and knowledge, experiences and skills, attitudes and beliefs, shared interests and values, perhaps in the same region and industry.

This example vividly demonstrates to you that the entrepreneur has the perceptions coming from the environment and their exact standard of the qualities which the team should possess. These are the perceptions of feedback from the social situation, and the criteria are an inextricable part of the entrepreneur's identity standard. Only the entrepreneur is in a position to compare the perceptions or feedback with the identity standard of what the team members should be.

That is why they are controlling perceptions or feedback and are responding to the comparison with the actions of finding people through a network of friends, significant others, and former colleagues from previous organisations or start-ups. *Others* in this example should suit the start-up entrepreneur as an individual, as a person. If the founder formed the right team, they would confirm their identity standard of success because they would think about themselves as being good at spotting talent.

To reiterate. The entrepreneurs were establishing their companies with a clear identity standard to create value not only for the customers but also for themselves. The meanings of how they saw themselves in their role influenced their strategic choices.

This takes us to the quotes from the entrepreneurs of different types. I would like you to carefully consider them to gain deep insights so that you could compare their identity standards yourself.

'Success' as the identity standard

Peter, a high-flyer identity: 'I think "success" is just being financially free. Just to be where I want when I want. And also, being able to work on things that I enjoy, not being dictated by a boss.'

Hugh, the lifestyle entrepreneur identity: '… I want a certain level of lifestyle. Nothing riches kind of thing – not a private jet; but I want a bit of certainty – a comfortable life.'

Colin, a high-flyer identity: '"Success" for me is a multifaceted thing; it's a skill set that you are always developing. It's about pushing yourself to improve your skill set, learning from your mistakes, developing your own self-esteem and your own character. Being true to your ethics, understanding what your values are and upholding those, adapting them.'

Derek, the lifestyle entrepreneur identity: 'I think for me personally, "success" is achieving what you set out to achieve while maintaining who you are and whom you want to be.'

Andrew, an inventor identity: 'Well, in the mid-term, to partner up with a big sort of utility provider ... to roll out our system on a larger scale. Sell a lot of systems and team up with somebody who is gonna enable that.'

Alan, a high-flyer identity: 'I think that the monetary side is definitely crucial.'

Peter, a high-flyer identity: 'Oh, the main frustration is that you wanna work a hundred miles an hour and you wanna take on the world, but you are surrounded by people who aren't bothered, and they are not hungry, and they wanna get home and watch EastEnders [a British TV soap opera]. So, you wanna go a hundred miles an hour, but to them, it's just another job; and they are not as passionate as you are, or they don't get the vision, or they don't buy it, or they don't want to innovate.'

By and large, the entrepreneur's identity standard of success may manifest itself when the entrepreneur is planning an exit strategy. The founder's decision to exit the company they have created is one of the most important ones. I would argue that it is also one of the most difficult because of the identity standard of how the founders see 'success'. Beyond everything, entrepreneurs do not care about the success of others; they care about *their* success. That is why it does not matter to entrepreneurs how other founders plan their exit strategy. They may look at it merely as guidance. What matters to *them* is *their* exit plan. The identity standard plays a crucial part in the decision-making process because it is more about the individual rather than a business.

Selling the business to another company or going public with an initial public offering (IPO) is the most commonly used entrepreneurial exit strategy. Some investors, however, disagree and do not consider the IPO an exit strategy. For them, it is just the next round of funding. Despite that, I would stick to the first definition to illustrate the operation of the entrepreneur's identity standard.

In this case, we may deal with a high-flyer identity or an inventor identity. Merging with another firm to reduce the level of uncertainty in their own business or selling the company may be a more cautious exit strategy. We may be talking about a lifestyle identity because the founder would not want to put their lifestyle at risk. However, not many entrepreneurs would think about declaring bankruptcy or selling an equity stake as a strategy.

That's where the identity-standard meanings of how one sees *their* success may hit. The identity standard may go wild, and the founder may experience sleepiness nights, feelings of failure, and grief about the loss of the venture. 'Why is this happening?' you may ask me. This is because the entrepreneur may have the IPO in their identity standard of success. At the outset, the IPO might have been the exit plan, but things have changed. The marketplace has changed, and the company has not adapted to a new game yet. But what about the identity standard of success? Has it changed completely or been modified somehow? Not at all. That is why it may drive the founder mad. 'Who am I now?' one may ask. 'A looser?'

Yes, it is hard. It does take courage to go through it and come to terms with a new situation. 'Why is it so?' I hear you probe. Since the meanings in the identity standard cannot change overnight, they may lead to all sorts of irrational decisions. The entrepreneur may think that they are acting in a certain way, whereas in reality, it is the identity standard of what success means to them that guides their actions. Of course, being unsuccessful is a sore point with entrepreneurs. Some may even find themselves to be on the verge of despair. In those circumstances, other people's reactions are usually difficult to accept. Therefore, the thoughts in the head created by the identity standard can become disruptive. They are hard to deal with, which makes the situation so tricky.

In extreme cases, entrepreneurs may be driven to suicide because their venture has failed. It is not their fault; it is the fault of their identity standard of what 'success' means to them personally. In other words, the accumulation of negative thoughts about oneself. The start-up founder may feel tired and demoralised, non-transparent because of the shame, and not committed anymore. After all, there is ample room for comparison with other start-up founders, and the fact that investors may not look kindly at a "failed" entrepreneur seems unbearable. 'How can I look them in the eye?' the founder may inquire.

They may lose their senses and not find their way out. The situation may utterly dash what optimism could have meant to them one day. And there is nothing to motivate them anymore. Emotions and tears may blur their identity standard of how they normally see themselves to be capable of setting up and running a venture. It is sad but understandable, given the operation of the identity standard: what it means to them to be an entrepreneur. After all, it is not *them*; it is the identity standard in them.

'Optimism' as the identity standard

Andrew, an inventor identity: 'I think we [I and my co-founder] have become increasingly optimistic about the industry. It's gonna be huge in the next five years ... we can both remain hugely optimistic.'

Hugh, the lifestyle entrepreneur identity: 'Well, obviously, I started very optimistically, and I got a bit deflated. There is a lot of complexity. I tried working with companies that were really cheap and overpromising. And they never delivered.'

Kevin, the lifestyle entrepreneur identity: 'We were quite realistic. I mean we were optimistic that it would be fun, and it wouldn't be stressful; we did realise that it would be *hard*. I think we made a fair assessment of how hard it was gonna be. But probably not the levels of stress that it could bring.'

'Motivations or capabilities' as the identity standard

Thomas, a high-flyer identity: 'I've been involved with several start-ups. I've seen the processes that are required in order to do that. Having gone through the process several times previously, I believe I am capable of doing it myself.'

Reynold, the lifestyle entrepreneur identity: 'Because I wanted to. I think at the point I was with my, you know, family situation. We were getting married and having a child and everything like this on the way; I wanted to find a more formal discipline thing.'

Ralph, a high-flyer identity: 'I've always been an enterprising fellow. So back at school, we used to run a family warehouse type of business. So, my family has always been in business.'

Philip, a high-flyer identity: 'Because of the skills I possess and my business partner, so both of us are complete as a whole.'

Luke, the lifestyle entrepreneur identity: 'It will allow to travel wherever I like, allow me to move to a different country and work from there or do whatever, so ... yeah.'

Carl, the lifestyle entrepreneur identity: 'From reading accounts of people who've done it. That was the main thing, really, when after a while I saw a door, "If they could do it, I could do it."'

Andrew, an inventor identity: 'The biggest key milestone was when I quit my job – my full-time job. So, there were two milestones. One – the decision. Two – the actual kind of throw myself into this fully. I suppose the next milestone was "Is this gonna work? Can we put something together that actually works?" And then the next milestone is "Are people gonna buy this?"'

Charles, the lifestyle entrepreneur identity: 'Well, obviously, the key milestone was leaving work. That was the first major decision. The second decision was ... bring the CTO on board and giving them an equity stake in the business.'

At this point, you may be wondering, 'Can the identity standard change?' Well, some scientists argue that it may take a decade for an identity to undergo a change. They often provide an example of an individual who discovers 10 years later that they are different. 'I wasn't like that 10 years ago,' they may say.

However, I would claim that the identity standard of an entrepreneur may never change. Their appearance might, but not their identity standard. For instance, if money and Lamborghinis are the measure of being successful, it may stay with the entrepreneur for the rest of their life.

I would argue that the modification of the identity standard – and, consequently, the identity itself – is hardly likely to happen on its own. Those founders who have experienced it, though, may say that their values have entirely changed, or they do not see money as the measure of success anymore. 'I am a completely different person now,' they may assert. But are they? What about their actions? Whom do they serve? Their former identity standard of success, perhaps?

If they act differently than they have done before, then their identity standard has changed. You may notice this if a high-flyer entrepreneur becomes a lifestyle entrepreneur or the other way around. Another example may be when an entrepreneur with an inventor identity becomes a high-flyer because the meanings of success or motivations have transformed. It's rather interesting, especially when you observe it in others and yourself. What makes them tick is what they have in their identity standard. That is all there is to it.

To conclude this chapter, I hope the examples I have provided to you so far have explained why entrepreneurs act in specific ways. Remember, entrepreneurs base their strategic choices on the comparative process of the feedback they receive from others in social situations related to them personally and what they have about themselves in their identity standard of success, optimism, and motivations or capabilities. That is why a high-flyer identity, an inventor identity, and a lifestyle identity tend to differ in this regard.

Chapter 4

STRATEGIC ACTIONS INSIDE A START-UP

Being a CEO is somewhat personal in nature because the fact that something works for me doesn't mean it will work for someone else.

–MATT BLUMBERG

Throughout my conversations with the entrepreneurs, I asked about how they made their strategic choices. These decisions were mostly related to the entrepreneurs' business practices which arose inside their ventures. For example, opportunity creation or recognition, finding start-up resources, and planning. A comparison occurred between what came from a social situation and what entrepreneurs held about themselves in their identity standard of success, optimism, and motivations or capabilities.

This section explains how and why it relates to the entrepreneur's business practices. I will show you how the variations in the identity standard of success, optimism, and motivations or capabilities affect their internal and external actions. I will also connect three different types of entrepreneurs to these internal and external actions.

Opportunity creation and recognition

My interview discoveries suggested that each entrepreneur viewed an opportunity in his own way. For example, Alan (a high-flyer identity), stated his approach: 'Initially, I will start [searching for opportunities] maybe from the internet or a referral from somebody.' As Alan illustrated, he always started online first or would prefer somebody to give him a contact. It seems that this kind of behaviour gave him control. It would also appear that an online search provided quick and easy access to the required information. In contrast, Keith (the lifestyle entrepreneur identity) took a different position on the same subject when he said: 'Go into conferences, networking, talking to people.' Keith was more outgoing and open. He believed in creating a business opportunity by talking to people directly at conferences. Maybe he experienced a sense of connectedness and cooperation when he attended those events, which proved to be stimulating and comfortable for him. This method of opportunity creation was undoubtedly in his identity standard of how to be successful.

Some tech start-up founders, however, differed in that respect because of other reason. Derek (the lifestyle entrepreneur identity) noted another issue:

> A lot of opportunities are coming our way. A flip side of that is trying to deal with opportunities that keep arising; maintaining focus on what we've achieved to be sustainable. So, I wouldn't say ... go and seek ... cause they are already planned or what we have access to.

Derek suggested that sometimes it was not necessary to seek opportunities himself, because he was overwhelmed by the sheer amount of them. And that was not his doing. Others were responsible for it, which limited his autonomy and led to ambiguity and complexity. That did not align with his values, and that was not how he pursued excellence. He wanted continuity of what he had achieved so far. It was in his identity standard of success and optimism to step aside and carry on with his daily work. It seemed right for his self-esteem and self-worth.

Carl (the lifestyle entrepreneur identity), however, mentioned something different in terms of his opportunities:

> I think I've been sort of following what people … following the need, really … following what people have said and trying to listen; reading between the lines.

As you can observe, Carl was always looking for opportunities when he had conversations with people. He expressed his creativity by seizing the initiative and analysing the information from others. It was easy for him. These were the meanings which he kept in his identity standard of success.

There were also start-up founders who valued conversations and introductions as a way of recognising opportunities. Ralph (a high-flyer identity), for instance, highlighted the following:

> It's through conversation … where most opportunities come through. The school of thought which I belong to says, "Tell every one of your ideas because you never know what conversation might spark what idea in your mind."

Visibility and networking were essential to Ralph. The very fact that he wanted to share his insights with others points to the meanings he had for himself in his identity standard of success and motivations or capabilities. Ralph was not afraid somebody would steal his ideas and execute on them. It shows his confidence because of these identity-standard meanings. Ralph believed in serendipity as a way of gaining fresh insights in order to refine his business concept.

As I have demonstrated to you, some start-up entrepreneurs seemed to be outwardly focused (e.g., networking, talking to others, and market research). In contrast, others seemed more internally focused (e.g., internet searches and evaluating opportunities brought to them).

The high-flyer identity entrepreneurs were engaged in online networking first. Perhaps it was because their identity was generational, and they already had the support of their families. These were their identity-standard meanings. They had the know-how, so they believed that online communication was most suitable in order to find new collaborators. Later, they would focus on face-to-face conversations to help them navigate their way through future uncertainty.

Whereas the lifestyle entrepreneur identity manifested itself in talking to people directly and concentrating on others who wanted to work with them. You could observe that some entrepreneurs with this identity type engaged directly with their customers. Generally speaking, these entrepreneurs intended to maintain the lifestyle that they already had, which was consistent with their interpersonal communication to establish contacts with others. They wanted stability and support to protect who they were – to preserve their identity.

Entrepreneurs with an inventor identity were doing market research and carefully considering their customers' and competitors' behaviours. This was their way of gaining a competitive advantage for brand positioning and a new product development. Being able to identify opportunities for disrupting the industry based on their analysis of the market revealed their entrepreneurs' identity and their identity standard even more. Maybe because the inventors loved puzzles and enjoyed solving problems.

Finding start-up resources

Throughout my conversations with the tech start-up founders, their entrepreneurial identity defined how they were searching for start-up resources. The identity standard of entrepreneurs' motivations and capabilities, as well as their standard of success, influenced their business practices. Stanley (an inventor identity), for instance, was direct in the way he confronted some of the common difficulties:

> This week has been quite difficult regarding speaking with investors and trying to make decisions. So I had to make a decision about whether it could affect the company in the long run with regard to share equity, finances, staff. Understanding whether Nick, my brother, would feel the same way when I actually made them. I wish he hopefully did.

As you can see, Stanley faced the decision of giving equity to his team members. He was concerned about how much stake each team member should own. Stanley wanted to make the right decision that would also satisfy his brother. Stanley was aware of his brother's identity standard of how to be successful. He knew what would motivate or incentivise his brother to carry on running the business and how much equity he would prefer to share with the investors. To confirm the meanings in his identity standard of success and motivations, he acted in a way to verify his brother's identity standard as well. It is called a 'mutual verification process'.

Additionally, start-up resources also involved focusing on the company's management team. Kevin (the lifestyle entrepreneur identity) noted the following: 'In terms of the directors – now it's just me. That was a key milestone: a good decision.' Kevin was satisfied with his own decision to be a director, which meant identity verification. Richard (a high-flyer identity) made a contradictory statement by saying: 'There is a time frame in the management board meeting between three directors and also the contractors: managing expectations.'

Richard was not the only director and preferred to have a board meeting between the other two directors and the contractors; to have everyone together. The entrepreneur was aware of his responsibility to report to a board of directors. He also received feedback from his contractors. It seemed that these meetings were the identity-verification response to how the directors should lead and manage each project.

Interestingly, learning how to deal with human resources was at the top of the agenda for Jack (a high-flyer identity):

> Obviously, employees are expensive. So, I won't see return on that investment there for three months, so massive involvement getting employees in, cause we have a three-month lack on that cash we have just spent on them. So, I would say *that* was the key point for us ... sorting out HR problems.

Jack was aware that human resource (HR) decisions made at an early stage could affect the downstream success of the start-up. Perhaps such decisions as recruiting, reward, compensation, promotion, and performance management in general were a real challenge for Jack because the company's money was tight. Despite the increased difficulty in recruiting and retaining employees, Jack was determined to handle HR problems. This way, he verified his identity standard of how to remain unbeaten in the start-up environment.

The other founder, Reynold (the lifestyle entrepreneur identity), proposed the following:

> If it's a commercial decision, it takes a different mindset. If it's an HR decision or a product decision, you have to analyse differently. The only common denominator in all of them is to do our metrics. That's what really aids a decision-making process.

As Reynold explained, the best solution to tackle the problems, including HR issues, was to do metrics. That is why quantitative data were crucial to his entrepreneurial identity to verify the meanings held in his identity standard of how to be successful in business.

As you have seen so far, these two start-up founders made informed decisions. They did not hire people on a whim but had distinct ideas of when it was (and it was not) an opportune moment to hire someone. They based their decisions on reliable data. Their actions seemed to be the opposite of Stanley's (an inventor identity) who made decisions based on agreement and conflict avoidance.

The above quotes have shown you that entrepreneurs were developing different strategies. At first glance, these strategic choices related to what was right for their business. But don't forget! They also referred to how they saw themselves as tech start-up founders — their entrepreneurial identity.

Some entrepreneurs were trying to find resources by engaging in information-seeking behaviour, looking at both competitors and customers. Keith (the lifestyle entrepreneur identity) supported this argument by saying:

> Competitors ... well, you know what you are trying to do. So, you try to find other people who are doing similar things. Look at their customer perspective and say, "Why would you then buy from that?" To do the research, I would pretend to be a customer ... go out into the marketplace, and ... it's articulating, "No, no, we are not doing that at all. We are offering this."

Keith was trying to engage in the process of finding useful resources for his venture by understanding what the demand and supply were. The founder always questioned himself about why others would buy from his competitors and what products customers wanted. By actively collecting information this way, Keith was confirming the subjective meanings in his identity standard of success about his abilities to introduce something new into the market and create value.

Similarly, Alan (a high-flyer identity) pointed out the following:

> If I've got a customer, they will come first. OK? Whether it's a negative on the balance of cash flow, whatever.

Despite the possibility of negative cash flow, Alan put his customers first. This demonstrates his commitment, reliability, and trustworthiness as a leader. These were his identity-standard meanings of how to be successful and control the growth of the company. Alan also added:

> I am very good at finding resources to do the job. Once you've taken the money off somebody, then it's your job to complete that contract. So, taking on people with demand, taking off people. I try very hard not to. I can go more without, personally even, that to get rid of someone.

By looking closely at what Alan was saying, you can notice his confidence about the skill set required for resource allocation and the performance of a particular task. It also signifies his intelligence. As I have mentioned earlier, all the entrepreneur's opinions or preferences or strategic decisions are being checked with the identity standard of success, optimism, and motivations or capabilities first. Taking more new people on board was not in Alan's identity standard of how to operate in the start-up environment. Dismissing someone would mean an error signal produced by the comparator in his head. These actions would be associated with identity non-verification or non-confirmation of his identity-standard meanings about achieving success. For this reason, Alan did his utmost best to avoid such situations, which in turn confirmed his identity standard of being capable of doing the deals without hiring additional employees. These were his identity-standard meanings of how to remain effective as a founder and CEO.

As I have just demonstrated to you, finding start-up resources mattered to each of these tech founders. The entrepreneurs arranged various of their business activities in a way that confirmed their identity standard of success, optimism, and motivations or capabilities, which verified their entrepreneurial identity.

The inventor identity entrepreneurs tried to speak to investors about how much capital they required for their venture — not surprising, bearing in mind their artistic nature and passion for innovation. It was their identity standard of motivations or capabilities. This type of entrepreneurs also talked about a shift from being employed to becoming tech founders. They made their decisions by reaching an agreement since they usually had low levels of optimism about their product. Their identity standard of success kept those meanings. Some of this type of entrepreneurs concentrated on finding the right team for the company's management by learning how to deal with HR problems.

The lifestyle entrepreneur identity allowed the founders to engage in information-seeking behaviour to find the necessary resources. Their identity standard of success meant financial security and personal independence.

The high-flyers were concerned about the right management team. They were as active as the lifestyle entrepreneurs in terms of information-seeking behaviour, but for different reasons: their ambition, determination, and high levels of optimism were in their identity standard of optimism.

Planning

A vast majority of the tech start-up founders believed in a general vision rather than a detailed plan. For example, Patrick (a high-flyer identity) shared his views by saying:

> I have a vision for three years, five years, and then I have a short-term vision for a month. We have a wall,

so we put all our ideas on Post-it notes, and we stick them on the wall. And every three months we put those Post-it notes in order. Some of that does to a business plan, but I know where I want to be.

Patrick's identity-standard meanings of achieving success revolved around either a short-term or a long-term vision. For instance, the start-up entrepreneur explained how the Post-it notes helped him detail and prioritise the critical milestones in his planning timelines. Ralph (a high-flyer identity) shared a similar approach to planning:

I often plan in big steps ahead, so I know I need to achieve this goal. I might not have the most detailed plan to get there; giving yourself the freedom to manoeuvre.

Ralph preferred not to describe what he wanted to achieve in minute detail because he did not like predictions. Instead, he believed in creativity and gave himself the freedom to plan for the future by confirming the meanings in his identity standard of success and optimism.

The flexibility of entrepreneurial activity allowed Ralph (a high-flyer identity) to prepare and implement a plan that suited him most. Such an adaptive approach was on display in the case of George (an inventor identity) as well. Alan (a high-flyer identity), for example, mentioned the following:

For me, I have to build the whole picture. If I can't see the whole spine chain, the whole sales process, the whole end game, then for me that's very boring.

Here the start-up founder wanted to see the process from start to finish and put all the pieces together first. Again, these were the meanings in his identity standard of how to be successful in running a start-up. You can now notice that George and Ralph attached value to flexibility, while Alan needed security. For that reason, Alan (a high-flyer identity) noted: 'Steps of different components and different income streams and different sections of the business to build everything else.'

While discussing the same subject of planning, some founders emphasised the role of an iteration. Thomas (a high-flyer identity) stated the following:

> You are constantly pivoting. It's a very iterative process. So, I mean, it's difficult to say how quickly or how far ahead we are able to plan and how closely we can follow that schedule. Our development of the product has pretty much stayed on schedule. In terms of other planning, it's been more of a flexible learning kind of schedule, rather than this has to be done by this time.

As Thomas articulated, the process of repeating the previous steps and learning from the results was significant for product development as well as other operations. He could not specify when he was ready to finish working on his product or how long the process would last. Thomas deliberately stated he wanted to have the same freedom. Other entrepreneurs wanted it too. This way, Thomas verified the meanings in his identity standard of optimism about the product. This optimism was not separate from him as the creator of the product.

Richard (a high-flyer identity) expressed similar views for learning:

> So, we are always creating a knowledge base. I am constantly learning from my own personal mistakes, and other people's mistakes cause we deal with contractors. So, to have "lessons learned" from other projects. It is really important. It's like a debrief. We do it with every job.

As a start-up leader, Richard thoroughly understood the importance of reflection and its impact on learning because he wanted to reach his potential. That is why he created a specific knowledge base for every project. Having done that, Richard was confirming his identity-standard meanings of success and motivations or capabilities.

Finally, some entrepreneurs explained why project-management tools were necessary for their planning. Hugh (the lifestyle entrepreneur identity), for instance, argued:

> It's very much like project management. So, I need to get everyone to work together, cause obviously, I need to build relationships with the retailers. That's probably the best example. With some of the retailers, I cannot really establish a relationship until we have the product up and running.

Hugh needed to use project-management tools to establish a strong relationship with the retailers. At the same time, the start-up founder implied the importance of maintaining relationships. Here you can see the identity-verification response of how Hugh saw himself in the role of the effective leader.

As a lifestyle entrepreneur, the founder expressed realism. His identity-standard meanings of success were inseparable from engaging in project management.

To conclude, it is best to refer back to some of the elements in the identity standard of success, optimism, and motivations or capabilities. I have identified these as crucial dimensions of the identity standard itself because the values entrepreneurs have about these three categories affect their business decisions and strategies. You have just seen it in my examples from the research data.

In this section, I have discussed how the high-flyer identity manifested itself by describing entrepreneurial actions. This type of entrepreneurs focused on a general vision rather than a detailed plan. They also concentrated on an iterative process, which went in line with their identity standard of success as self-development and constant learning. But do not forget! Typically, these entrepreneurs know what they want and believe they can get there. Their identity standard embeds all these meanings.

Interestingly enough, the inventors – those with the inventor identity – admired the flexibility of entrepreneurial activity, which allowed them to plan as they wanted. The lifestyle entrepreneurs, however, used project-management tools to build relationships with individual companies because their identity-standard meanings often contained financial security. In general, they needed to build strong relationships to maintain a particular lifestyle. They wanted certainty, which they believed could only come from working together with established companies. The lifestyle entrepreneurs avoided focusing entirely on their venture. Again, working with established companies implied less uncertainty and a concentrated effort, which would give them autonomy and more flexibility in terms of personal time. These were the meanings in their identity standard of motivations and capabilities.

Chapter 5

STRATEGIC ACTIONS OUTSIDE A START-UP

The earliest phase is usually the most productive.

–JESSICA LIVINGSTON

When I asked my tech start-up founders about strategic decision-making or actions outside a start-up, they described what their decisions involved. In particular, finding collaborators, involvement in the tech community, making a social impact, and developing a reputation. This chapter is designed in a way to help you understand how the identity standard of success, optimism, and motivations or capabilities is associated with these activities.

Finding collaborations

I identified significant differences between the start-up entrepreneurs when I asked them about how they found people to collaborate with for their businesses.

One of the reasons for being enrolled in the incubator programme was wide exposure to new opportunities, networks, and various sources of information about tech. For example, Jack (a high-flyer identity) shared his experience: 'Just here [the incubator]. I meet everyone that comes into here. You just generally open a conversation with them. We also have a kind of expert sessions.' For Jack, one of the primary purposes of being in the incubator environment was to meet new people. They could potentially benefit his business because they were also starting their ventures. Charles (the lifestyle entrepreneur identity) supported these views by saying: 'Very good, actually. Especially in this environment [the incubator] ... other start-ups based as well. I find it very encouraging.' Being in the incubator's social environment provided a much-needed boost to Charles's confidence to carry on with his business. His identity standard of motivations or capabilities was verified by being among others who were in the same boat. The meanings of his identity standard revolved around inspiration, comfort, and fulfilment.

As the above examples illustrated, finding collaborators involved others outside the founders' circles. The identity-verification process, through the confirmation of the identity-standard meanings of success, appeared to be the same. For instance, the above quotes suggested that by being in the incubator environment, the entrepreneurs confirmed their entrepreneurial identity and seemed to be delighted with their choice of the tech incubator. In my experience, there was no one who regretted having joined the hub. There was enough adaptability within that social environment to go about one's own business and decide how much you want to interact with others. It inspired confidence and eliminated vulnerability.

Some tech start-up founders highlighted the aspect of finding people outside the incubator. Charles (the lifestyle entrepreneur identity) mentioned the following: 'There are various meetup groups for entrepreneurs and start-ups within this area of the

UK. Those are the forums to kind of communicate.' Charles described how forums outside the incubator community were just as active, whereas Norman (the lifestyle entrepreneur identity) made a different point: 'Emm … finding people is the hardest thing. So, it's all been by personal contacts. That's how I've found everyone I am working with.' Norman's identity standard of success was that personal contacts were the best for doing business. He also admitted how challenging it was to find people. His identity-standard meanings of relying on those he had already known and respected guided his actions. Maybe he had worked with those people before and recognised them as colleagues. Perhaps they were just his loyal and trusted friends. Either way, Norman's identity-standard meanings of being surrounded by people he knew guided his actions on how to hire the right talent for his business to thrive. It boosted his senses of safety and security as well as his confidence. He did not want to put his identity at risk by working with strangers.

Ralph (a high-flyer identity) was the same in that respect: 'So, with employees, it's often based on folks I know.' Despite the differences in Norman's and Ralph's identities (a lifestyle and a high-flyer respectively), they had identical identity standard regarding talent. They wanted to work with whom they had already created alignment because it gave them certainty and predictability regarding work ethic. These meanings were deeply ingrained in their identity standard of success.

There were also the founders who mentioned the aspect of a 'mutual benefit'. Jonathan (a high-flyer identity) expressed that in the following way:

> If I help people, those people probably gonna help me. I'd say I have a very good network of people whom I try

and help. I went down to N accelerator to mentor, and I met a team … partner with them … beneficial to us … beneficial to them.

As you can see, Jonathan knew that he had the knowledge and the experience, which were needed to collaborate with others. He was sure of what exactly he could give in return. The meanings of the identity standard of success contained Jonathan's expectation or experience of reciprocity. He was aware that personal relations (i.e. a network) were an essential resource for his business. The entrepreneur acted because of that experience. Not surprising, considering he was a mentor on one of the incubators that helped already established companies improve their growth.

Other founders preferred to find interns for their business. For example, Thomas (a high-flyer identity) shared his views:

A couple of work experience programmes that we work with, a couple of internship programmes. Several universities and government organisations, schools as well – to get our A-workforce.

As you can see, Thomas was trying to get first-class employees by being in touch with schools and universities through internship programmes. It was his way of confirming the meanings in his identity standard of the role of the successful leader: the meanings of how to run a profitable start-up by attracting specific human capital.

Stanley (a inventor identity) was the same in that respect. He said: 'When we try people in-house, we are going to go for universities, go to graduate sites, elementary recruitment agencies.' Stanley illustrated the same approach to finding the right employees for his start-up. These two tech founders believed that educational institutions were an essential part of their network, connected to their HR practices. From this, I want you to see that there is a connection between internal actions inside a start-up and external actions outside that start-up.

Perhaps the ideas of recruiting interns by going through those institutions came from what they learned when they studied at university. Or maybe they learned this technique from other entrepreneurs and their best practices. Perhaps they had positive experiences with recruits from these places in the past. From what I could observe in these entrepreneurs, they valued the interns' enthusiasm, knowledge, and passion for what they were developing. Probably an important factor was that the university itself was a stone's throw from them in terms of geographical location. So, naturally, they wanted to exploit that kind of opportunity to their advantage.

Lastly, some entrepreneurs expressed concern about finding collaborators on the internet. Matthew (an inventor identity) explained: 'Prefer to work with companies we can speak with and actually meet face-to-face rather than other companies on the internet.' Alan also made an interesting point:

> I think, get out into people's faces, you know. If you are kind of person that is not face-to-face – you are more of a technical person – then you might struggle with people skills in that respect.

People skills were highly valuable for Alan because they helped him talk to others directly. It was his way of building rapport and trust with people. Again, this is confirmation of his identity-standard meanings of success.

To sum up, the high-flyers were using the incubator programme to find others for their business. Having said that, they were always in contact with a professional network outside the incubator. Remember, this type of entrepreneurs was ambitious, and they wanted high status. Some of them continued the family tradition of running a business. Moreover, they knew that their knowledge and experience would be beneficial to others, including their business colleagues. Also, the high-flyers were in touch with universities through internship programmes.

The inventor identity entrepreneurs were close to the high-flyers, as they preferred to find interns for their ventures. In general, founders with an inventor identity tended to express low levels of optimism about their product, which would explain why they believed that graduates with fresh ideas could meaningfully contribute to their businesses. They tried to build trust through face-to-face interactions because it was in their identity standard of success to be known for their product by communicating its benefits.

The lifestyle entrepreneurs either used meetup groups to find collaborators or preferred personally trusted contacts.

Involvement in the tech community

I found that the degree of community involvement varied among start-up founders. For instance, Scott (a high-flyer identity) argued:

> Heavily involved. So, within the tech community, I've always been to lots of different events; I know quite

a lot of faces and can always have conversations with everybody. Within the website [the actual business], I kind of manage all our community site. So, I need to be speaking to people to find out what's going on on the site.

Scott made two rather interesting points. Firstly, he mentioned his active involvement with other individuals in the tech industry. Secondly, the founder pointed out his collaboration with others, possibly technical or non-technical people, on his website. Both activities closely intertwined with each other and represented the meanings in his identity standard of success. Scott felt comfortable with either action, which also confirmed his identity standard of motivations or capabilities. He knew well that in order to be successful in business, he should be as active as possible. That was Scott's identity; that was how the founder saw himself in his role of the entrepreneur. He possibly wanted high status and manifested his ambition this way as a high-flyer.

Other entrepreneurs, however, were involved in the tech community only to a certain extent. For example, Norman (the lifestyle entrepreneur identity) said:

Moderately. Back in N (a city in the UK), I was a lot more involved than I am now … there is a lot of meetups, conferences, people … talk about their products. Just constantly there, really. But now I am … walking away … come down to the bootstrapping side of things. Clients happy on the one side – then build my own things on the other side.

The meanings of Norman's identity standard of success had changed because the entrepreneur had moved away from the tech scene and was more focused on the business side. You can observe the recollections of his recent years when he appeared to be an active member of various tech events. Even though Norman's identity standard of success had changed over the years, the entrepreneur verified his identity of being successful again by being less involved in the tech scene. Whereas some years ago, Norman had confirmed his identity-standard meanings of success by being heavily involved in the tech community.

Now you can see with ease how the founder's entrepreneurial identity changed at the time. Perhaps this had happened because the entrepreneur had realised that he could be successful without events, constant buzz, and pressure. It is also possible that the start-up founder could not combine a demanding schedule of meetups and tech conferences with a daily business routine. Despite that, Norman's identity did not suffer in the slightest.

Luke (the lifestyle entrepreneur identity) supported this view by adding: 'To be honest, I am not involved, really. I am focusing all my time on this [his business].' The same as Norman, Luke tried to focus heavily on his start-up. He was protecting his identity by not participating in a range of tech events. Reynold (the lifestyle entrepreneur identity) made an interesting comment in that respect by saying:

> A lot of it comes down to, I think, the time constraints. In terms of the tech community, the whole aspect of disruption here. I've got a wife, I've got a child, young child. And *that* combining with my close friend network is, for me, personally, more than enough in terms of a community.

Limited community involvement was related to Reynold's schedule when the founder considered any further participation as disruption. It reflected how much he valued the relationship which he had with his family and friends. Stability and fulfilment were the meanings in his identity standard of success. For these reasons, he did not feel guilty. It is also possible because his identity type (i.e. a lifestyle identity) does not usually have high growth aspirations.

Let's now look at the bigger picture. The inventors with an inventor identity focused on educating others about entrepreneurship – they wanted to share the experience of solving problems, which was their identity standard of how to be successful in tech. The high-flyers were doing it as well. They were also heavily involved in their tech community. Usually this type of identity wants high status and seeks confirmation from others. In contrast, lifestyle entrepreneurs were only involved in the tech community to a certain degree. And this is true because typically they love autonomy and want to keep the lifestyle they already have.

Making a social impact

This theme was about the social impact that the start-up founders thought they had from their business. They took different positions on the subject. George (an inventor identity) mentioned the following: 'I'd like to meet some people who are interested in starting businesses and reaching out to people, a lot of people at school ... teach how to be more entrepreneurial.' As you can see, George wanted to be more involved in teaching others about entrepreneurial activity, taking responsibility for transferring knowledge about entrepreneurship; educating others. The founder selected schoolchildren as the right audience for his talks to verify his entrepreneurial identity. This type of audience was of specific relevance to him because the founder believed that it was better to learn about entrepreneurship at an early age. George's identity standard of motivations or capabilities contained those meanings. The founder knew that knowledge of entrepreneurship gained at a young age is a prerequisite of becoming a successful entrepreneur in the future.

Patrick (a high-flyer identity) had similar ideas. He replied, 'So, at the moment I am helping university and college students learn about entrepreneurship and help start their own businesses.' Patrick helped university and college students know more about what entrepreneurial activity entails. These were his attempts to confirm his identity-standard meanings of success as an entrepreneur. Why? Because he was able to pass on his wisdom. It also showed that he took pride in leading a start-up. Both George and Patrick were verifying their identity-standard meanings of success by ensuring that young people gain exposure to the entrepreneurial mindset through such communication with them.

Reynold (the lifestyle entrepreneur identity) highlighted the aspect of charitable work when he said: 'If we can partner with that, develop that and help … do something like that for non-commercial reasons.' From what you can see, Reynold wanted to partner up with an organisation to help people in need. Even though Reynold was at the beginning of his entrepreneurial journey, the importance of charitable giving was in his identity standard of success and possibly motivations.

Kevin (the lifestyle entrepreneur identity) expressed similar views: 'We are *definitely, definitely* looking at … once we are kind of established and profitable … doing charitable work.'

From what you can observe, Kevin prepared himself to give back to society through donations to charities, as long as the start-up gained legitimacy and reached a certain level of profitability. These views may refer to the identity-standard meanings of what motivated both individuals beyond monetary considerations.

Other entrepreneurs, however, emphasised the significance of entrepreneurship from an inspirational perspective. As Alan (a high-flyer identity) put it:

> Well, obviously, I've helped twelve hundred people in my community get into work, so people find it aspirational from, you know, lower sectors: catering, security, bus driving. Allegedly low sectors to then being self-employed, being flexible to work, have less overtime, being able to have holidays when they want and not to have a boss, in terms of real-life value.

This compelling argumentation pinpointed several aspects at once. First of all, Alan stressed how many people he was able to help through entrepreneurial activity. It was crucial for his identity, especially his identity standard of what motivated him. Secondly, he was proud of being an entrepreneur because he could potentially fulfil the aspirations of so-called 'lower sectors'. He talked about the value of freedom in terms of independence, flexibility, and autonomy for these sectors in society. For Alan, entrepreneurship was a way of providing jobs and creating growth. These were the meanings in his identity standard of success as well as the identity standard of motivations or capabilities. The activities which Alan described motivated him in his pursuit of helping others while feeling good about himself. Whereas Scott (a high-flyer identity) argued:

> Communities are all about sharing. Right? I have
> a heightened system willingness to give. So I started
> a company called Health First, which is a socially-
> focused company working with people with different
> food allergies and intolerances ... helping people.

Scott was driven by social causes when he started a company,
which focused on helping individuals with certain medical
conditions. The founder's actions as the output to the
environment demonstrated a solid attempt to verify his identity
as the social entrepreneur. Helping people was in his identity
standard of motivations. To put it differently, these were Scott's
motives.

Finally, making a social impact was straightforward for Gregory
(an inventor identity), who said the following:

> So, for us, it's really clear. We are working in education;
> we are specifically aiming at school kids. So, if more
> kids get more GCSE grade C in English and Math,
> more kids will get better jobs and have a brighter future.

Gregory was working on an educational product for
schoolchildren to improve their chances to do well in exams.
In all likelihood, this was a purpose of running a business for
him. Maybe it was about his responsibility or capability to
help kids who had problems at school. Again, the meanings in
his identity standard of motivations influenced his actions or
strategic choices.

To sum up, lifestyle entrepreneurs expressed a keen interest in
charitable work because their meanings of 'success' were partly
based on financial security and partly depended on helping

others. The high-flyers thought their entrepreneurial activity already inspired others to follow in their footsteps. Perhaps that was because their ambition came first. However, they were also concerned about social causes and making the world a better place.

Finally, the inventors were creating value for schoolchildren because they were concerned about their progress, performance, and future career opportunities. These reasons motivated them as they were in their identity standard of motivations or capabilities. Furthermore, they were passionate about their software innovation because they loved puzzles and enjoyed solving problems. Due to their abilities, they genuinely wanted to help children achieve good grades and become qualified for better competitiveness in the modern workforce. Indeed, the inventors' identity standard of success held these meanings.

Developing a reputation

Contradictions existed in how entrepreneurs viewed 'reputation' and its development concerning their own identity. For many of them, 'reputation' was not just about developing the right product or offering a reasonable price. It was about their associates and clients. It was about being seen as producing a good and honest product as well as building a genuine relationship with other people. It was about the skill of communicating well.

Kevin (the lifestyle entrepreneur identity), for example, focused on various aspects simultaneously when he said:

> We are quite lucky actually to work with companies which are … like multi-million-pound turnover

companies. So, established companies but not famous ones. I am currently chatting to mentors about it [developing a reputation] at the moment; it's how to differentiate yourself. On the product side of things, it's all about realising that first gaming product – a successful one. On the client side, getting in sort of well-known brands or clients and doing the work well, getting it upon your website.

There were several aspects of Kevin's identity here. First of all, despite having a successful product, the entrepreneur emphasised how 'luck' played a part in bringing them projects from well-known companies. The tech founder cherished the fact that he was one of the fortunate ones. It offered him validation of his business concept. Secondly, Kevin started having conversations with mentors about how to stand out as a business. Such actions verified the founder's identity of doing the right thing for himself and his company. They confirmed the meanings in his identity standard of success and optimism.

Some entrepreneurs were trying to build trust with others. Stanley (an inventor identity) explained his position:

So, we will really like to crack down on bullying and data and hopefully grow our trust base with users. Reputation in terms of product in the social industry, it's a trust thing, really.

Stanley suggested changing the users' perceptions of social media by dealing with bullying and improper data usage. This clearly demonstrates that trustworthiness and integrity were his key priorities. Consequently, ethical behaviour was at the core of Stanley's identity. Another start-up founder, George

Some tech founders were not sure about their reputation. When I asked Carl (a lifestyle identity) whether he knew what his reputation was, he said the following: 'He-he. Probably not. I mean, I still feel I am faking it; I haven't made it yet. Maybe people in the tech community admire what I am doing.' For Carl, it was still early days to be known as a business. He had not confirmed his identity standard of success yet. It showed a non-confirmation of Carl's entrepreneurial identity because he had not confirmed the meanings of how he imagined himself in the role of the tech founder. Despite that, the entrepreneur hoped others in the tech community respected him for his work.

That discrepancy between the feedback he received from others from the surrounding environment and the meanings of success in his identity standard was not very large. It seems Carl had probably received some positive feedback from others in the tech community regarding his progress and competence. It partly confirmed his identity-standard meanings of success. The founder was more inclined to think he was faking whatever he was doing. Therefore, it gave rise to the sense of not being there yet, which is a clear sign of the disconfirmation of his identity standard of success.

Similarly, Norman (the lifestyle entrepreneur identity), made a noteworthy comment by saying:

> I don't think I do have much reputation for previous work. I needn't say that if these products are building on quite well, I don't think it would happen either. Because it's very much behind the scenes kind of thing.

Despite building the right product, Norman did not believe in the development of a reputation that way. It was a 'private' thing for him. The tech founder valued the standing with a small circle of insiders more than his reputation to the outside world. It resulted in the business practice of working on the products to earn the reputation as a good leader 'behind the scenes' — his identity-standard meanings related to not being publicly known. Norman felt comfortable with his situation. He didn't expect overnight popularity because he did not need it; he was complete in his role of the entrepreneur. He was already successful and verified his identity standard of success.

To recap, what I have shown you is that lifestyle entrepreneurs emphasised working with well-known companies or clients to earn a reputation. It came from their standard of success based on financial security and a degree of personal independence from their business. They saw it as a stable solution where they needed to spend less effort adjusting to the unpredictable.

The inventor identity entrepreneurs were trying to build trust with others by managing expectations. Their high perceptions of risk associated with their innovation. Despite being fundamentally optimistic about innovating, they were more cautious and realistic about their products. They worked hard to persuade others about the selling points. It is also in line with their identity standard of success of being known for their products. The inventors worked efficiently and effectively with others and wanted to be known for that.

The high-flyer entrepreneurs were developing a personal brand through public speaking. Usually, this type of founders is ambitious and expresses high levels of optimism that they demonstrate to others. If we compare, the lifestyle identity was more about ensuring product quality. In this, their behaviour was similar to some high-flyers. However, other lifestyle entrepreneurs were not sure about their reputation. It may be because such type of individuals does not have high growth aspirations in their identity standard of success and often expresses ambivalence.

Chapter 6

THE POINT OF NO RETURN

I think in my twenties I tended to think of all people as sort of more or less alike. Now think that people are really different in all these subtle ways that are very important.

—PETER THIEL

At the beginning of 2020, the COVID-19 crisis was quite unprecedented and hit the whole world hard, which was beyond anything that could conceivably have been imagined. It had changed the perceptions, views, and norms of the start-up ecosystem, including founders and owners, financial institutions, the investment communities, and the entrepreneurial spirit as a whole.

Many technology start-ups had gone bust because of the lack of cash, no further capital available at short notice, and drastic changes in their team structures, which then led to job losses. Markets' requirements had become more sophisticated in their need for entirely new and even more innovative business models. Some entrepreneurs argued that social norms had changed too.

Game-changing solutions always take time to occur and evolve into viable products or services to be accepted by the markets. Therefore, it seems that post-COVID-19 crisis consumers will demand fresh approaches to customer care and problem-solving. Furthermore, employee engagement and loyalty are at stake because of high expectations of health and safety standards and companies' compliance with the related government regulations.

Start-ups and the entrepreneurs who build them are the engines of a healthy society. That is why this book aspired to attract your attention to the entrepreneur's identity and spark your interest in the entrepreneur's identity standard by supplying you with useful tools for better reasoning. I hope you have already felt a shift in your understanding of what entrepreneurs think about themselves and why. I wanted to make you more aware of the tech founders' strategic actions because they are inseparable from who they are and what's important to them. For you, this shift is just the point of no return.

I wanted you to become more alert. I wanted you to know that the entrepreneur's identity and the meanings contained in a given identity standard of each leader is part and parcel of their decision-making processes. It is not mere speculation; this is a fact supported by the research data. It is evidence-based since most of the start-up founders in my book were from one UK tech incubator programme.

 I have provided various examples of how tech start-up founders were trying to confirm the meanings held in their identity standard of success, optimism, and motivations or capabilities. Likewise, I showed you how entrepreneurs tried to verify what they thought about a particular decision, which inescapably touched on their sense of self. I introduced and described in minute detail three types of entrepreneurs according to the meanings they held about themselves in their identity standard of success, optimism, and motivations or capabilities. These types were the 'high-flyers', the 'innovators', and the 'lifestyle' entrepreneurs.

I should remind you some of the start-up founders may have the characteristics of two or even all these types. The main point of such a typology was to show you what distinctions could exist between the entrepreneurs and their identity standard of success, optimism, and motivations or capabilities. Again, I have designed it in a way to help you identify each identity standard.

Hopefully, you are now able to see for yourself how the meanings which entrepreneurs gave to themselves led to specific actions. To put it differently, my book explored how the entrepreneur's identity standard of success, optimism, and motivations or capabilities guided the activities inside and outside a venture. Efforts inside the start-up included opportunity creation or recognition, looking for start-up resources, and planning. Actions outside the start-up manifested themselves in finding collaborations, involvement in the tech community, making a social impact, and developing a reputation.

Just a few final words. I have written this book for you, and I believe that it has served you well in the pursuit of a rewarding experience. I wanted my ideas to be exciting and thought-provoking. So, I hope I've hit the nail on the head about the importance of the entrepreneur's identity standard and their identity in general.

Every action that a start-up founder takes has consequences. Eventually, identity and the entrepreneur's identity standard of success, optimism, and motivations or capabilities affect actions, which in turn influence the entrepreneurs' productivity and the performance of those around them. Consequently, it relates to whether a venture pursues or does not pursue growth in the future. For these reasons, sustaining rapid growth or, come to think of it, any growth may pose a problem for the start-up entrepreneur because of the operation of their identity.

It is by no means certain that by considering the quotes of the founders from the tech start-up world, you have already become much more profound. I would urge you to reflect on my views and apply ideas I have outlined for you in real-life situations. A word of caution, however. Be extra vigilant because *your* identity standard of success, optimism, and motivations or capabilities will serve as a basis for how you see other founders and possibly yourself. This book has provided you with vital examples to recognise these identity standards on your own. Once you observe anything resembling what I have shown, you'll know the reasons for others' actions and respond to the arising circumstances with this new understanding of the entrepreneur and his or her role in the social structure.

Finally, I believe that my book has helped you build resiliency and continuity, especially during this challenging post-economic shutdown period, to take appropriate actions and be confident about them.

ACKNOWLEDGEMENTS

I should acknowledge that the scientific basis of my topic is identity theory. It comes from the works of two academics: distinguished professor emeritus of sociology, Professor Peter J. Burke, and Professor Jan E. Stets, both from the University of California, Riverside. Professor Jan E. Stets is also director of the Social Psychology Research Laboratory (SPYRL) at the same university.

Of course, I'd like to extend these thanks to my literary agent Publishizer. Had it not been for your tech company, I would never have got access to the self-publishing industry. The connection with eBooks2go and my editor, David Baker, is a consequence of everybody's efforts from such a fantastic high-tech start-up, especially Lee Constantine and my scout, Julia Guirado, for being professional and approachable. The same goal motivated us all: to find the right publisher and get things going. You do an incredible job for all authors because of your vision of what a fruitful collaboration between agents, editors, and authors should look like in the age of technological disruption. Thank you for your passion – keep it up!

Beyond the shadow of a doubt, the publication and the release of the book could not have been possible without Leslie Chirchirillo, John Bean, and other team members from eBooks2go. I wanted my manuscript to be meaningful for those who could see the value in it. I am proud of having eBooks2go as my self-publisher because you are truly exceptional. You treated my work with care and attention, which I will never forget.

Last but not least, I am incredibly grateful to a large number of authors in the tech industry for their insightful books, from Ben Horowitz and Scott Belsky to Jerry Colonna, Rand Fishkin, Maynard Webb, Noam Wasserman, Simon Sinek, Tim Ferriss, and Seth Godin. You gave me a real inspiration to transform my academic contribution into a non-scientific endeavour. I am deeply indebted to your wise words for helpful clues. Above all, I truly appreciate the scale of work involved, which shines through every page of your books.